WEATHER

Written by
Tony Potter

Illustrated by
Robin Lawrie

Designed by
Teresa Foster

Consultant editor
Dick File

London Weather Centre

CONTENTS

About this book

Every day there are hundreds of weather forecasts – on TV, radio, in the newspapers and on special weather phone lines. The weather is in the news too, with devastating hurricanes, terrible droughts and even gloomy stories of how the weather is changing. Some say the weather is getting hotter, others that it is getting colder...

This book is a guide to the basics – from why it rains to how hurricanes are formed, with a look at just what might happen in the future. You can find out how the weather affects our lives – and animals' lives too. There are facts and records and explanations of amazing weather tricks. There is even a weather station of your own to make!

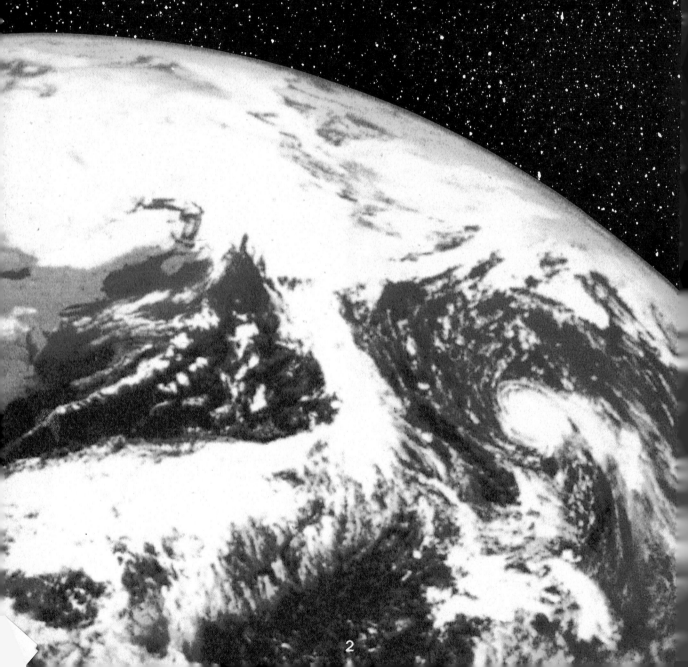

A view of Earth's weather from a weather satellite

What is weather?

Weather is the wind, the sunshine, the rain and the snow. It's the cold that numbs your toes and the heat that warms your body. To scientists, weather is the state of the air, or atmosphere, at any particular time or place.

In some places, the weather is much the same day after day. In other places, such as Britain, the weather changes so much that it is difficult to tell what will happen even a few hours ahead. The usual pattern of weather in one place is called its climate.

Weather is an endless cycle of events – from clouds, snow and rain, to lightning, hail and hurricanes. All these are made from three basic ingredients constantly at work like a giant machine in the atmosphere: water, wind and heat from the Sun.

The weather machine is very complicated. Scientists, called meteorologists, study the weather to understand how the machine works. All round the world, 24 hours a day, meteorologists record what is happening to the weather. From this they are able to make forecasts of how the weather is going to change.

Weather words

This book introduces many weather words. You can check what they mean on page 47.

Where does weather happen?

The Earth is surrounded by a thin layer of gases that protect us from extremes of heat or cold. These layers are called the atmosphere. The lowest layer is called the troposphere. This is where all the weather happens.

Satellites

Stratopause

Stratosphere

40km

30km

Ozone layer

The weather only happens up to this height.

20km

Concorde

Tropopause

Airliner

Highest clouds

10km

Troposphere

Mount Everest

Bird

Sea level

Living with the weather

The weather affects your life in many ways – it controls what you wear, the kind of things you eat and even the things you are able to do. You can usually plan ahead, at least a day or so, because of fairly accurate weather forecasts. But there is still little anyone can do to control the weather.

Ancient times

In ancient times the weather was thought to have magical or religous powers. People prayed to the gods for sun and rain to help make their crops grow. The ancient Greeks, for example, had weather gods, such as Zephyrus, god of the west wind and Boreas, god of the north wind. Even today, American Indians, some African tribes and Australian aborigines have tribal "rain makers" who perform ceremonies to make the rains come.

A rain dance.

Bad weather

The weather can affect the way people behave. Teachers often think that children, for example, are bad-tempered when it is very windy. In France, it is even said that the Mistral wind can make people go mad! Riots too, are thought to be more likely to happen when the weather is very hot and humid. Some of Britain's worst riots have happened in this kind of weather.

Feeling low

Many illnesses are made worse by the weather. People with chest ailments suffer more when the air is cold and damp with fog, for instance. Hay fever is a problem in the summer when dry weather helps pollen from flowers and plants fly easily into the air.

Technology beats the weather

Technology sometimes gets round the effects of the weather to enable people to do what they want. For example, ball games such as soccer are played in wet weather – on plastic grass! See how many other examples you can think of where technology beats the weather.

Weather sayings

Weather sayings are simple weather forecasts which have come about over hundreds of years by people watching the weather. Some are still useful today because they are quite accurate.

Red sky at night, shepherd's delight, Red sky in the morning, shepherd's warning. (English saying)

This saying means that a sunset is usually followed by a dry night, but rain is on the way if the sky is red in the morning.

Mackerel sky and mares' tails, Make tall ships carry low sails. (English saying)

"Mackerel sky" and "mares' tails" describes kinds of clouds which sometimes bring strong winds.

A sun shiny shower, Won't last half an hour. (English saying)

Check for yourself if the sun shines during a shower to see if this saying is true.

Christmas on the balcony means Easter in the embers. (French saying)

If it is warm at Christmas, Easter is likely to be cold.

Shelter

All round the world people protect themselves in different ways from the wind, rain, Sun and snow. The weather affects the clothes you need to wear, the kind of house you live in, and even the kind of car you have.

Clothes

The picture on the right shows clothes you might wear in winter or summer. Your body is always trying to keep you at an even temperature. Clothes help by protecting you from the weather.

Your body protects itself too. If you are cold your muscles twitch and make you shiver to keep warm. If you are hot sweat on your skin dries and cools you down.

Winter

- Umbrellas are a simple way of keeping dry.
- A quilted coat traps air inside to keep you warm.
- More heat escapes through your head than any other part of your body.
- Your hands and feet lose heat quickly. Gloves and thick socks in your boots help to protect them.
- Wellington boots were named after the Duke of Wellington, who wore long black boots.

Summer

- The Sun sends out rays. Some of these can be harmful, but there are ways of protecting yourself from them.
- A hat helps to keep the Sun's rays from your head. Too much heat on your head can make you ill.
- Sunglasses cut down the Sun's glare.
- A loose skirt and shorts trap cool air inside them.
- Suntan oil protects your skin from the Sun's harmful rays.

Houses

People have found ways of making their homes comfortable whatever the weather is like. The shape of your home and the things used to build it are all affected by the kind of weather where you live.

The Bahktiari people in Iran stretch their tents over low stone walls. The wind blows through the sides to keep them cool.

Houses in many hot countries are painted white to reflect the Sun's heat and keep them cool.

Loft insulation helps stop heat from escaping upwards.

Air conditioner

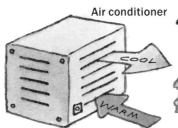

Double glazing helps stop heat from escaping through the windows.

Some people keep their homes cool with a machine called an air-conditioner. This cools the air as it sucks it in from outside.

Homes in Europe and the USA are protected from the cold by trapping warm air inside. This is called insulation.

Cars

Anti-freeze liquid

In cold countries cars need special liquid in the radiator to stop the water inside freezing in winter. Hot-air heaters keep the passengers warm.

Cars in hot countries need special filters to keep dust out of the engine. A filter is a bit like a sieve. Air-conditioners keep the car cool inside.

Wildlife and the weather

The weather affects animals in many different ways. Some animals, like hedgehogs, go to sleep for the whole winter to escape the cold. Others, like lizards, need the warmth of the Sun to make their bodies work. Farmers especially have to pay attention to the weather to make sure their animals are well protected.

Winter sleep

Some animals find life difficult in the winter. There is very little food around, so animals such as hedgehogs, tortoises and doormice, eat as much as possible in the autumn. They live off their fat by sleeping for the whole winter in a warm place. This is called hibernating.

A hibernating animal's temperature drops to match its surroundings and its heart beat slows right down to save energy.

When it is frozen, birds such as robins cannot dig their beaks into the ground to find worms and insects to eat.

Hill farmers often lose sheep in deep snow drifts. Sheep, like the one in the picture above, manage to stay alive for days under the snow until they are dug out.

Birds find it difficult to get a drink when it is icy because they cannot peck through the ice. It is a good idea to leave a dish of warm water out for them.

Hibernating hedgehog

In harsh winters, such as in 1987, helicopters are used to airlift food to horses and cattle stranded in remote areas.

Fly away

Some birds fly away to warmer places in the winter. This is called migrating.

In December or January, Gulls, Lapwings, Woodpigeons, Robins, Thrushes and Starlings fly to Britain if it is very cold in Norway, Sweden and Denmark.

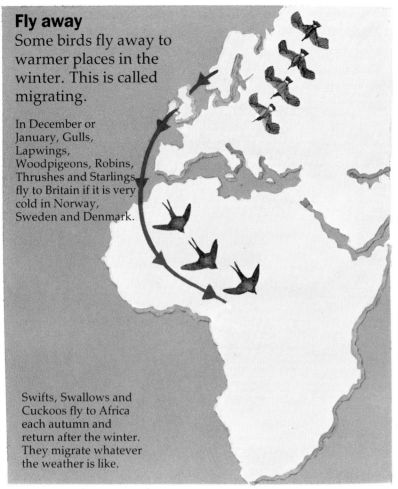

Swifts, Swallows and Cuckoos fly to Africa each autumn and return after the winter. They migrate whatever the weather is like.

Animal migration

Animals as well as birds need to migrate. Waterbucks in Southern Africa, for example, migrate to wetter areas during the dry season.

Hot dog

On a hot day, you will see dogs panting. Dogs cannot cool down by sweating, but lose heat through their tongues instead.

Lizards

Lizards and other reptiles are cold-blooded. They need heat from the Sun to warm up. When it is cold they are not very active.

Wet birds

Birds hide in hedges and under bushes when it rains. They keep warm by puffing up their feathers to insulate themselves.

Climate

Each area of the earth has a certain kind of weather, from scorched deserts and steamy rainforests to lush pastures and fertile valleys. The pattern of weather these places expect from year to year is called their climate. Some places, such as the Antarctic, have very extreme climates – the temperature there is below freezing even in summer. Other places, such as Britain, have very mild climates because the weather is neither very hot nor very cold.

Different climates

The world is divided into different types of climate, shown on the map below. The climate depends on how far somewhere is from the equator. This distance is called latitude and is measured in degrees. Climate also depends how far somewhere is from the sea and on its position on a continent.

Tropical grasslands and monsoons: very wet or very dry.

Polar: cold, ice-covered lands, some snow in the Antarctic, but less in the Arctic.

Temperate: changeable weather, usually with warm, dry summers and mild winters.

Desert: very little or no rainfall. Little variation in weather between the seasons.

Mountain: colder the higher up you go.

Cold forest: very cold in winter, hot in summer.

Rainforest: hot and wet all year round.

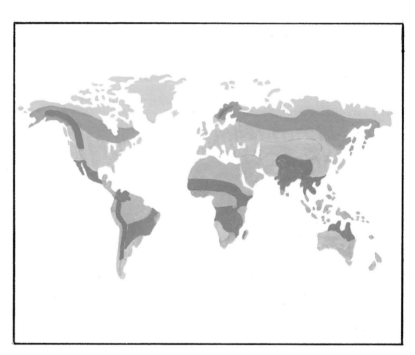

Odd climates?

Moscow and Edinburgh are on the same latitude, but the climate is very different. This is because Edinburgh is near the sea, while Moscow is hundreds of kilometres from it. Places near the coast are called maritime climates. Here, the temperatures stay fairly even through the year because the sea temperature does not vary much.

Edinburgh is warm in summer and mild in winter.

Moscow is very hot in summer and freezing cold in winter.

Country climates

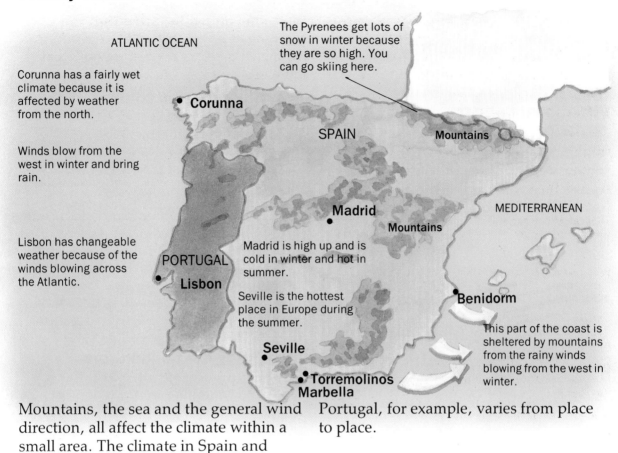

ATLANTIC OCEAN

The Pyrenees get lots of snow in winter because they are so high. You can go skiing here.

Corunna has a fairly wet climate because it is affected by weather from the north.

Winds blow from the west in winter and bring rain.

Lisbon has changeable weather because of the winds blowing across the Atlantic.

• Corunna

SPAIN

Mountains

• Madrid

Mountains

MEDITERRANEAN

Madrid is high up and is cold in winter and hot in summer.

PORTUGAL
• Lisbon

Seville is the hottest place in Europe during the summer.

• Benidorm

This part of the coast is sheltered by mountains from the rainy winds blowing from the west in winter.

• Seville

• Torremolinos
Marbella

Mountains, the sea and the general wind direction, all affect the climate within a small area. The climate in Spain and Portugal, for example, varies from place to place.

Microclimates

Scientists call the climate in very small areas a microclimate. A microclimate can be the size of a city or as small as a back garden! The examples below show how different the climate can be even within a tiny area. This affects the kind of plants that grow, or the sort of animals you find.

Gardens

In Britain, south-facing walls are the warmest spot in a garden because they are sheltered and get the sun all day as it passes from east to west.

Mountains and hills

The bottoms of valleys are always protected from strong winds, but can be in the cold shadow of the surrounding hills. Hilltops are exposed to strong winds, making it difficult for trees to grow.

Cities

Cities are often much warmer than the surrounding countryside. All the concrete stores the Sun's heat during the day, warming the air at night.

Hot and cold

Whether you feel hot or cold depends on lots of things – the strength of the wind or the clothes you are wearing, for example – but most of all it depends on the amount of heat from the Sun. The warmth you feel is called the temperature.

Day and night

The Earth spins round once every 24 hours. Daytime is where the Sun is shining onto the planet. The Earth absorbs energy from the Sun and gives it out as heat. Much of the heat you feel actually comes from the Earth and not the Sun.

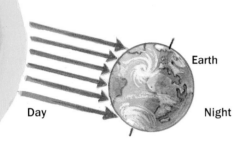

Day   Earth   Night

The Sun warms the surface during the day. It starts to get cooler at sunset.

At night, the surface gradually loses its warmth. The coldest time is at dawn, just before this side turns to face the sun again.

Sunsets

A sunset happens when the Sun goes behind a hill or a mountain as the Earth spins. Sometimes you can see the Sun shining on a cloud after it has gone down.

Why are the poles cold?

The Sun's rays hit the Earth in straight lines, as shown in the picture. Because the surface is curved, the rays spread out more at the poles than they do at the equator. This makes the poles much colder than the equator.

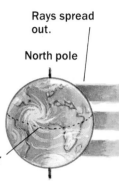

Rays spread out.

North pole

Equator

South pole

Measuring the temperature

Temperature is measured with a thermometer in units called degrees Centigrade or Celsius. A small bulb at the bottom contains a liquid which expands, or gets bigger, as it gets warmer. The liquid is forced up the glass tube and you can read the temperature marked beside it on a scale.

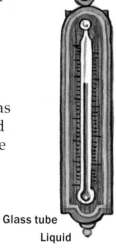

Glass tube

Liquid

A Swedish man called Anders Celsius introduced the Centigrade scale (°C) in 1742. Gabriel Daniel Fahrenheit of Germany invented the Fahrenheit scale (°F) in 1718.

The seasons

The Earth takes one year to go round the Sun. The seasons of spring, summer, autumn and winter are caused by different parts of the Earth being tilted towards the Sun as the Earth goes round.

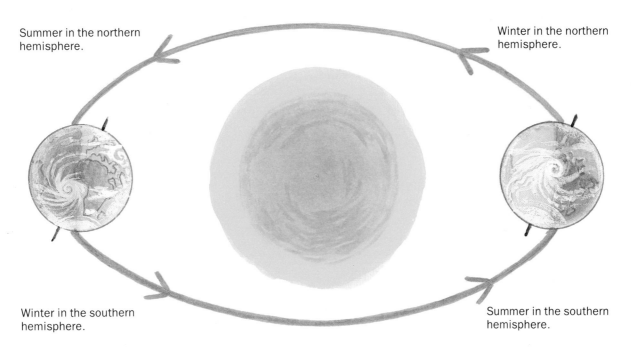

Summer in the northern hemisphere.

Winter in the northern hemisphere.

Winter in the southern hemisphere.

Summer in the southern hemisphere.

The North Pole is tilted towards the Sun.

The North Pole is tilted away from the Sun.

Hottest place on Earth

The hottest place on Earth is Dallol in Ethiopia. The average temperature in the shade is 34.4°C.

Coldest place on Earth

Vostok, near the South Pole, is very cold. The temperature is often minus 70°C. Even a home freezer is much warmer!

Pressure

The weight of all the air in the atmosphere pressing down on everything is called air pressure. The pressure varies constantly from place to place, getting higher or lower, and bringing different kinds of weather.

High pressure areas usually have settled and sunny weather, while low pressure brings clouds and rain. The differences in pressure also decide which way the wind will blow.

The weight of air

An Italian, called Evangelista Torricelli, first discovered that air had weight in 1604. Try this simple experiment to prove that air weighs something. Tie two balloons to a stick as shown in the picture, then pop one of them with a pin. What happens to the other balloon? Can you think why?

Blow up the balloons so that they are about the same size.

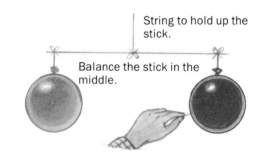

String to hold up the stick.

Balance the stick in the middle.

Pressure and height

Air pressure gets lower the higher up you go. The pressure at the top of a mountain or around an aircraft, for example, is much lower than at sea level. The picture below shows why this happens. The top cylinder stays round, but the others get more and more squashed by the weight of the others above.

Make six paper cylinders and push them onto a knitting needle.

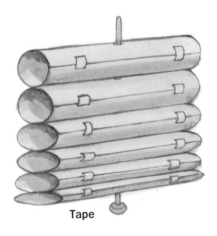

Tape

Air pressure varies at different heights because of the weight of air pressing down.

Aircraft cabins are specially pressurized so that people are safe inside.

There is less oxygen to breathe the higher up you go.

The air pressure at sea level is just over 1kg per square centimetre. Imagine a bag of sugar pressing down on every square centimetre of your body to get an idea of how much the air above you weighs. You don't feel this weight because the air inside your body balances the pressure on the outside.

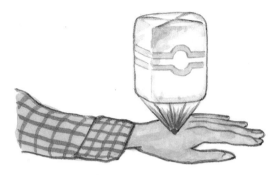

Hot air

Air pressure not only changes with height, but with temperature too. The warmer it gets, the less air there is. This affects the pressure. Some areas of Earth get hotter than others, so there are different areas of high and low pressure – and these are constantly changing.

More heat from the Sun reaches areas of the earth clear of cloud. This changes the temperature and the pressure in that area.

The temperature over the sea is warmer than the land in winter, but colder in summer. This makes the pressure vary between land and sea.

Highs and lows

Weather forecasters gather measurements from all round the world and make maps of the pressure areas. These are called highs and lows. Highs are areas where the pressure gets higher towards the centre, and lows are where it gets lower. If you stand with your back to the wind, the nearest low is on the left in the northern hemisphere and on the right in the southern.

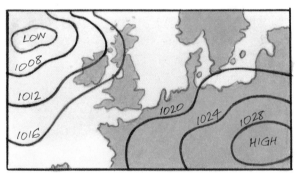

The lines on these maps are called isobars. The pressure is the same all along the line. The numbers on the map show the amount of pressure.

Barometers

Pressure is measured in units called millibars with a barometer. If you have one at home you can tell if a high is on the way when the pressure starts to rise, or a low if it falls.

See how to make a barometer on page 41.

Wind

The air around the Earth is always moving – across the surface of the planet and up and down too. Wind is air moving from one place to another. Sometimes you can tell where the wind has come from. Strong winds from the Sahara desert, for example, sometimes pick up dust and blow it thousands of kilometers to Europe. The dust is often left on cars and even colours the snow in the Alps.

What makes the wind blow?

A constant movement of warm and cold air makes the wind blow. The heat from the sun warms up different parts of the sea and land. These in turn warm the air above them. Air that is warmed becomes lighter than the surrounding air, so it rises. In other places, the air cools. Cold air becomes heavier, so it sinks. The wind blows because the cold air moves to replace the warmer air.

Masses of air

There are huge areas of air, called air masses. They are warm, cold, dry or moist depending on the land or sea they pass over. Boundaries between air masses are called fronts. There is usually wet, cloudy weather where cold and warm fronts occur.

Air in a heated room circulates in the same way as the wind moves.

Cold air

Warm air

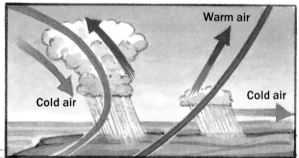

Warm air

Cold air

Cold air

Wind direction

You can see the direction of the wind by looking at a weather vane on a tower or church. A weather vane is made to point in the direction from which the wind blows. Wind direction is always given by saying the compass point from which it is blowing.

A wind sock is used at airfields to show the direction and strength of the wind.

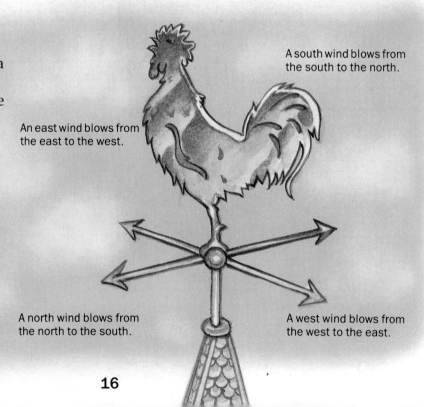

A south wind blows from the south to the north.

An east wind blows from the east to the west.

A north wind blows from the north to the south.

A west wind blows from the west to the east.

Wind speed

In 1805, Admiral Sir Francis Beaufort worked out a scale for measuring wind speed at sea. His scale is still used today, but has been altered for use on land.

Force 1 (2-5kph)
Light air

Smoke drifts but wind vanes do not move.

Force 2 (6-11kph)
Light breeze

Leaves rustle and wind vanes move.

Force 3 (12-19kph)
Gentle breeze

Leaves and small twigs move.

Force 4 (20-29kph)
Moderate breeze

Dust raised, small branches move.

Force 5 (30-39kph)
Fresh breeze

Small trees with leaves sway.

Force 6 (40-50kph)
Strong breeze

Large branches move. Phone wires whistle.

Force 7 (51-61kph)
Near gale

Whole trees sway.

Force 8 (62-74kph)
Gale

Twigs break off trees. Walking difficult.

Force 9 (75-87kph)
Strong gale

Chimney pots brought down.

Force 10 (88-102kph)
Storm

Damage to buildings. Trees uprooted.

Force 11 (103-120kph)
Violent storm

Widespread damage.

Force 12 (over 120kph)
Hurricane

Whole area devastated.

Beach breezes

Winds often begin near the sea. You can feel this sometimes when a cool breeze blows from the sea to the beach. On a hot summer day, the land warms up more quickly than the sea. Air above the land rises, so cooler air from the sea blows in to replace it. The wind blows in the opposite direction at night because the land cools more quickly than the sea.

Using the wind

People used to use the wind to power windmills, but in most countries today it is more often used to turn giant propellors to generate electricity.

Windmill still in use in Greece.

What is a cloud?

Clouds are made up of billions of tiny droplets of ice or water. Being in a cloud would be just like being in fog. In fact, fog is a cloud formed near the ground.

Each cloud droplet is smaller than a speck of flour. The droplets are so small and light that they fall slowly enough for the air to hold them up.

How clouds are made

Clouds are condensation, formed when warm air rises and is cooled below a certain temperature, called its dew point. This happens in the same way to condensation forming on a window or a mirror in the bathroom.

Clouds of dust

Water droplets in a cloud float much like dust. You can see this effect by closing the curtains in a room on a sunny day and letting a shaft of light shine through.

Warm air cools on the cold glass and condenses to form water droplets.

Heavy curtains

Dust floating around.

Flying through clouds

Pilots often fly right through the clouds to bright sunshine above. This picture shows cumulus clouds from a plane window.

Ten cloud types

There are three basic families of clouds, called cirrus ("curl of hair"), stratus ("layer") and cumulus ("heap"). They were given these Latin names by Luke Howard in 1804. There are seven other main types of clouds made up of combinations of these families. The kind of clouds you see give clues about the weather.

Clouds

Cirrus
Stratus
Cumulus
Cirrostratus
Altostratus
Nimbostratus
Stratocumulus
Cirrocumulus
Altocumulus
Cumulonimbus

See if you can identify these clouds:

Cirrus

Stratus

Cumulus

Cirrus are thin clouds, often called "mares' tails". After fine weather, they may show stormy weather on the way.

Stratus is a low grey blanket of cloud which often brings drizzle. They often cover high ground and cause fog.

These clouds look like giant puffs of cotton wool. Each may hold 1,000 tonnes of water – the same as 200 fully grown elephants.

Cumulonimbus are the most impressive clouds. They tower up to 15km high, almost twice as high as Mount Everest. Often they contain over half a million tonnes of water – enough to fill 125,000 buckets! They are a sure sign of rain, but not necessarily over you.

These clouds often look like a giant anvil.

Cumulonimbus means "heaped rain cloud".

Why different clouds?

Different sorts of clouds are formed because air rises for different reasons.

Air can be warmed by a small area of ground – fields heat more quickly than forests, for example. The air rises, cools and condenses to form a cumulus cloud. This process is called convection.

When air is blown against a hill it is forced to rise over the top. Often, this cools the air enough to form a cloud.

If a large amount of cold air meets warm air, it flows under the warm air and forces it upwards. This often forms stratus clouds.

Why does it rain?

Three main things are needed to make rain: plenty of moisture in the atmosphere, deep clouds (such as cumulonimbus or nimbostratus) and rising air. The word precipitation is sometimes used for rain, snow or drizzle.

How it rains

Scientists think that tiny water droplets in the cloud stick to floating particles of dust or salt.

The water droplets are constantly moving. They bump into each other and gradually get bigger.

Larger droplets start to fall, gathering smaller ones on the way, gradually growing bigger and falling faster.

As the raindrop falls, its shape is like an orange flattened at the bottom and not like a tear-drop, as many people imagine.

Raindrops

Surface tension

You can see the surface tension of water if you fill a glass almost to overflowing.

A raindrop can be up to about 8mm in diameter – the size of a pea. The raindrop is held together by its surface tension. This is like a "skin" on the water. The surface tension breaks above this size and smaller drops are formed.

Measuring the rain

Rainfall is measured with an instrument called a rain gauge. They have been used since the 15th century to keep records of the amount of rainfall each day. The simplest sort is a funnel in a marked container. The pictures below show how to make your own.

1
Pour water to a depth of 20mm in a wide jar.

2
Pour the water into a narrow jar. It will come much higher up.

3
Tape a piece of paper to the jar and mark off ten equal divisions.

4
Fix a funnel in the jar, sealing it with Plasticene.

5
Place above grass level so water will not splash in and affect your readings.

Read measurements in millimetres.

Showers and rain

Sometimes it pours for hours, but at other times there is just a quick shower. Air rising slowly over a large area will make it rain for several hours, but when the air rushes upwards over a small area there will only be a shower. The picture below shows how long rain or showers will last.

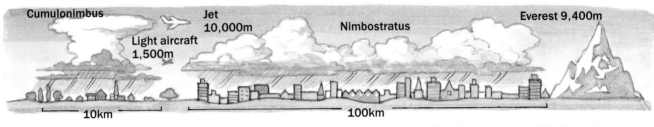

The cloud passes at 20kph, so the shower lasts for 30 minutes over the village.

The cloud passes at 20kph, so the rain lasts for 5 hours over the town.

The importance of rain

People need rain for drinking water, for their animals and for growing crops. Terrible droughts, caused by a lack of rain, strike many areas of the world each year.

Drought in Ethiopia in the early 1980's caused famine amongst millions of people.

The water cycle

Water is constantly on the move in a process called the water cycle. The same water goes round the cycle over and over again.

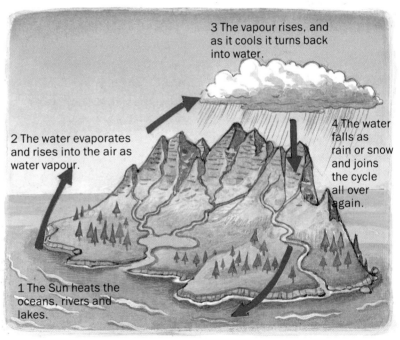

3 The vapour rises, and as it cools it turns back into water.

4 The water falls as rain or snow and joins the cycle all over again.

2 The water evaporates and rises into the air as water vapour.

1 The Sun heats the oceans, rivers and lakes.

GREATEST RAINFALLS				LEAST RAINFALLS		
Continent	mm each year	place		Continent	mm each year	place
Oceania	11,684	Mt Wai-'ale-'ale, Hawaii		S. America	0.8	Arica, Chile
Asia	11,430	Cherrapunji, India		Africa	2.5	Wadi Halfa, Sudan
Africa	10,277	Debundseha, Cameroon		N. America	30.5	Bataques, Mexico
S. America	8,991	Quibdo, Colombia		Asia	45.7	Aden, South Yemen
N. America	6,655	Henderson Lake, British Columbia		Australia	119.3	Millers Creek
Europe	4,648	Grkvice, Yugoslavia		Europe	160.0	Cabo de Gata, Spain
Australia	4,496	Tully, Queensland		Oceania	226.0	Puako, Hawaii

Thunder and lightning

Thunderstorms happen when large amounts of warm moist air move upwards very quickly – often on a summer afternoon. You can see a storm forming when cumulus clouds grow quickly into cumulonimbus clouds, the skies darken and the wind starts to blow. A thunderstorm, with heavy rain, thunder and lightning, will often only last for an hour or so. Each day there are thousands of them raging somewhere around the Earth!

Warm air moving upwards very quickly – a storm starts to form.

What causes lightning?

Violent air currents blow up and down inside a cumulonimbus cloud, forcing water droplets and ice crystals to crash into each other. Scientists think this creates friction between all the particles, causing static electricity. Each water droplet in the cloud is charged with either positive or negative electricity.

Sheet lightning

You see sheet lightning as a glow in the clouds. This is caused by sparks jumping between the positive and negative charges within the cloud.

Positive charges of electricity build up at the top of the cloud, negative charges at the bottom.

The ground is charged with positive electricity. There is an electrical "gap" between the cloud and the ground.

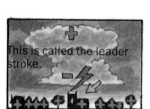

This is called the leader stroke.

The difference between the positive and negative charges gets bigger and bigger, until a spark jumps the gap.

Another stroke returns from the ground to the cloud. Both strokes happen so quickly that you see them as one.

What is static electricity?

Static electricity is electricity at rest, waiting to move. You can create it by rubbing a balloon on synthetic fabric. The electric charge will make the balloon stick to a wall. Try this in the dark and you may see sparks of electricity jump from the balloon to the wall.

What is thunder?

Lightning heats the air in its path to 30,000°C – five times hotter than the Sun's surface. The air expands and moves faster than the speed of sound, causing the crashing noise of thunder. Thunder and lightning happen at the same time, but light travels faster than sound, so you see the flash before you hear the thunderclap.

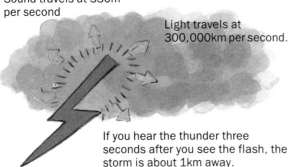

Sound travels at 330m per second

Light travels at 300,000km per second.

If you hear the thunder three seconds after you see the flash, the storm is about 1km away.

Crazy experiment

In an 18th century storm, Benjamin Franklin flew a kite dangling a metal key. He wanted to prove that there was electricity in storms, but his experiment was very dangerous because electricity is attracted to metal. He invented the lightning conductor in 1752.

Am I safe?

Buildings are sometimes damaged and people injured or killed by lightning. Lightning takes the shortest and quickest path to the ground, usually to a high object standing alone.

Lightning strikes aircraft, but the people inside are safe because it runs round the outside.

Lightning strikes lone trees on high ground – don't shelter here!

You are safe inside a car. The electricity is carried to the ground through the tyres.

If you get stuck in the open, make yourself low by crouching down or run for shelter.

You are safe indoors.

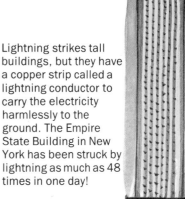

Lightning strikes tall buildings, but they have a copper strip called a lightning conductor to carry the electricity harmlessly to the ground. The Empire State Building in New York has been struck by lightning as much as 48 times in one day!

Dew, mist, fog and frost

Dew, mist, fog and frost are all the result of water vapour being in the air, cooling down and condensing (turning back to water or ice). There is always moisture, or water vapour, in the air – even in deserts. You can see the water vapour in your own breath condense on a cold day, as clouds of "steam" as you breathe out.

Wet air

The warmer the air, the more moisture it can hold. At 20°C, for example, the air can hold four times as much water vapour as air at 0°C. The air in a small bedroom might hold about a cupful of water.

The dew point

Air is a bit like a sponge. A sponge in a bowl of water will soak up the water until it can hold no more. Saturated air can hold no more water vapour. The temperature at which this happens is called the dew point. If the temperature drops below this point, the excess water vapour condenses to form water droplets.

Dew

On a calm, clear night, heat escapes quickly from the earth and air close to the ground cools below its dew point. The water vapour in the air condenses onto cold surfaces, such as grass, plants and cobwebs, and forms dew. The dew evaporates, or turns back to water vapour, as the air warms during the day.

Mist and fog

Condensation in the air near the ground forms mist or fog. This often happens in the evening as the ground is cooling. The cool air is heavier than the warmer air above, so the mist tends to gather near the ground or in valleys. To weather forecasters, mist becomes fog when they cannot see anything more than 1km away.

Contrails

Have you ever wondered about the white trails left in the sky by jets? These are called contrails and are caused by burnt jet fuel, which includes water vapour, condensing and freezing into ice crystals. This usually happens if the jet is flying above 10,000m.

Rime

The water droplets in fog sometimes freeze when they touch cold objects, such as trees and power lines. This is called rime.

Frost

If dew freezes after it has settled, it is called hoar frost. This makes beautiful fern-like patterns on windows. Frost can also form directly if the ground is already below 0°C.

Smog

Smog like this was called a "pea-souper"

1950s

Today

Many cities of the world have terrible smog. Smog is a mixture of fog and smoke particles. The pictures above show what London was like before smokeless fuels were introduced.

Ice and snow

Water freezes to ice when its temperature drops below 0°C. Ponds freeze over and roads become very dangerous. Black ice is even worse. This name is given to ice that you can hardly see on the road. It can be caused when it rains and freezes soon afterwards.

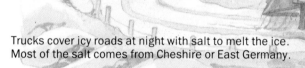

Trucks cover icy roads at night with salt to melt the ice. Most of the salt comes from Cheshire or East Germany.

Ice experiment

As it freezes, water expands by about 9%. Water pipes burst in winter because the ice splits the pipe. This experiment shows what happens:

1 Fill a plastic bottle to the brim and replace the cap.

2 Put the bottle in a freezer for a few hours.

3 The bottle will have split when you take it out.

Don't use a glass bottle.

Hailstones

Hail only falls from cumulonimbus clouds. Particles of ice are blown up and down inside the cloud, gradually getting bigger as they collect more layers of ice on the way. Eventually the hailstone drops out of the cloud.

Icebergs

Icebergs are giant slabs of ice that break away from the polar ice caps in warm weather. They float because ice is lighter than water. In the early 1980's scientists planned to tow an iceberg to Saudi Arabia and Kuwait to use for drinking water, but the plan was abandoned.

The most famous iceberg was one which sank the SS Titanic in 1913.

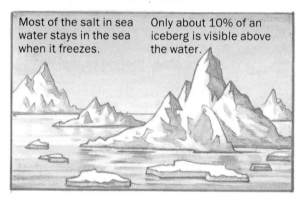

Most of the salt in sea water stays in the sea when it freezes.

Only about 10% of an iceberg is visible above the water.

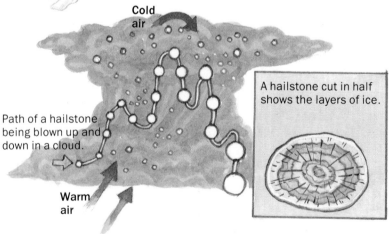

Cold air

Warm air

Path of a hailstone being blown up and down in a cloud.

A hailstone cut in half shows the layers of ice.

Snow

Snow crystals are formed in a cloud where the temperature is well below freezing point. They are made by water freezing onto ice particles. As a crystal falls through the cloud it hits others and becomes a snowflake. The air has to be below freezing too, or the snowflake will melt and turn to rain.

Flake shapes

Snow flakes are always six-sided and no two are ever alike. Their shape depends on the temperature – needle and rod shapes are made in colder air, while more complex shapes are made in warmer air.

You can collect snow flakes to look at under a hand lens on a piece of black paper.

Different snow flake patterns.

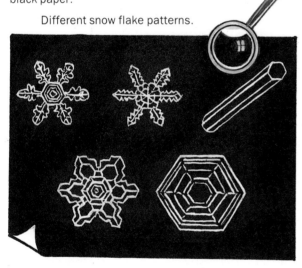

Old ice

Scientists can find out about past weather by drilling holes in glaciers and pulling out long plugs of ice. The plugs are layered and they can tell how cold the weather was by testing each layer.

Snow experiment

Fill ten empty yogurt pots with fresh snow without squashing it down too much. Let it melt indoors and see if you can work out how much snow you need to make one yogurt pot full of water.

Answer: About 10 yogurt pots of snow make one pot of water.

Snow drifts

Snow can get very deep by being blown into drifts by the wind. In 1917 there were 25m drifts in parts of Ireland – deep enough to cover a six storey building!

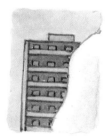

Trees are specially planted to help stop the snow in its tracks.

Avalanche!

An avalanche is when thousands of tonnes of snow fall from the side of a mountain, crashing into the valley below. An avalanche can be started by skiers, a thaw in the snow, a strong wind, or a heavy fall of fresh snow sliding across old snow.

Hurricanes and tornadoes

Hurricanes are incredibly destructive storms which usually begin over warm parts of the world's oceans. A hurricane generates as much energy in one second as ten atomic bombs. The wind is strong enough to demolish houses and whip up vast waves which destroy boats and harbours. Hurricanes last between two and five days and are called different things in each area, as you can see on the map on the right.

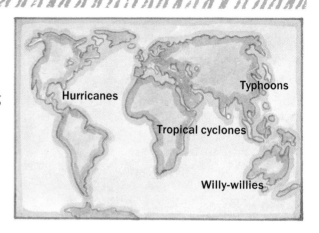

How a hurricane is formed

1 Winds going in opposite directions meet over the sea where heat from the Sun evaporates huge amounts of water.

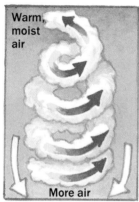

2 The warm air rises and more air rushes in to take its place. It goes around and up in a spiral.

3 Gradually, the wind blows faster and faster until it reaches anything between 118kph and 320kph.

4 The hurricane moves westwards and is usually about 300km across. Some hurricanes never reach land.

Hurricane names

When a hurricane is spotted it is given a name to identify it. The first of the season begins with an "A", the next a "B" and so on. This was first done in the last century by Clement Wragge, an Australian weather forecaster.

Worst hurricane

The worst hurricane was in Bangladesh in 1970, when about one million people were killed by flooding. In 1975, the city of Darwin, Australia was flattened by Hurricane Tracey.

Hurricane hits Britain

On 16 October 1987, a very severe gale hit southern Britain and northern France, with very little warning. The winds were as strong as a hurricane, between force 10 and 12, but the gale was not a true tropical hurricane.

This is a satellite picture of a hurricane. In the centre is an "eye", where the weather is calm, with light winds and clear skies. There is a lull in the storm as the "eye" passes overhead.

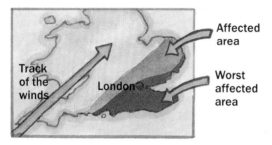

Affected area

Track of the winds

London

Worst affected area

The gale began off the coast of Portugal. Weather forecasters under-estimated the strength of the wind because of a lack of weather reporting ships in the area.

Track of the winds

Portugal

The gale caused massive damage. Over 13 million trees were uprooted, homes were wrecked and without power for days, and cars flattened. Thirteen people were killed. Trees were uprooted because the ground was so wet.

Tornadoes

Tornadoes, or "twisters", form over land and last between 10 minutes and four hours. They are more violent than hurricanes, but much smaller. A tornado is caused by clouds condensing and sucking a funnel of air into the sky. Winds swirl at up to 500kph along a path about 100 metres wide, causing total devastation.

This picture shows a tornado swirling over Australia.

A tornado leapfrogs across the land, sucking up anything in its path when it touches the ground.

Tornadoes are most common in central USA.

Weather tricks

The weather can cause odd effects, from rainbows to red snow and even hails of fish and crabs falling from the sky! Many effects are common and caused by tricks of the light. Others, like reports in the USA of a tornado picking up a railway engine and turning it round, are unlikely ever to happen again.

Rainbows

Rainbows happen when it is raining and the Sun is shining at the same time. You must have your back to the Sun to see a rainbow. Rainbows form a complete circle, but only part of it is seen from the ground. You can see the whole rainbow in an aircraft, mid-way between the rain cloud and the ground.

Red is on the outside.

Violet is on the inside.

Make a rainbow

You can make a rainbow with a garden spray on a sunny day. Stand with your back to the sun and look through the mist.

About light

Sunlight is made up of seven colours – red, orange, yellow, green, blue, indigo and violet. These are called the colours of the spectrum. Normally, you don't see them individually.

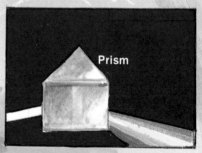

Raindrops are able to split sunlight into the colours of the spectrum, and reflect them to the ground.

Raindrop

You can see the rainbow most clearly against a dark-coloured background.

Why is the sky blue?

The Earth's atmosphere contains countless billions of molecules. When rays of sunlight shine through them, some of the blue light from the spectrum is scattered, making the atmosphere look blue.

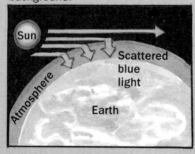

Sun

Scattered blue light

Atmosphere

Earth

If the atmosphere is very polluted, then more of the other colours of the spectrum are scattered. This makes the sky look milky white – often very noticeable over England, Central Europe and northeastern USA.

Haloes

Sometimes, for a few minutes, you can see a halo round the Sun or Moon. You can usually reckon on it raining within a few hours if you see one. These are caused by sunlight being bent through ice crystals in clouds high up.

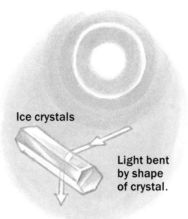

Ice crystals

Light bent by shape of crystal.

Mirages

Mirages are often seen over hot deserts or roads. They are optical illusions, caused by light being bent as it passes from a layer of cold air into a layer of warm air. The warm layer makes the light bend and you see a mirror image of the sky, which looks like water.

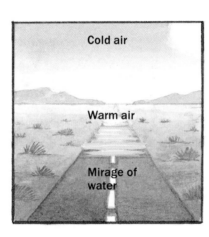

Cold air

Warm air

Mirage of water

Coloured snow

Snow in the Alps is occasionally pink, brown or even red! This is caused by coloured dust from the Sahara Desert being swept high up and carried 2,000km by the wind.

There are tiny bugs living in the snow above 3,000m which can also turn the snow pink.

Owzat!

An umpire at a cricket match in 1975 had his false metal leg struck by lightning. He was unhurt, but his knee melted and the joint stuck together!

Ouch!

Giant hailstones, the size of tennis balls, fell in Alabama USA in April 1988, smashing car windscreens.

Raining fish

Waterspouts are like tornadoes over the sea, and last for about an hour. They are swirling columns of air that suck up seawater and even fish and small crabs. Sometimes a waterspout moves onto land and the animals rain down!

Storm cloud

Anticlockwise swirl

Moves forwards at about 20kph

Several waterspouts were seen in the English channel on 18 August, 1974.

31

Disaster

Each year there are extremes of weather which bring disasters all round the world. Some cause millions of pounds or dollars worth of damage, but others leave people homeless or even dead.

With planning, some of the effects are sometimes avoided. In the USA, for example, the weather service tries to give up-to-the-minute warnings of approaching tornadoes so that people can take cover.

Too little water

Unexpected drought is a serious problem in many parts of the world. In 1976 the worst drought on record affected California, Britain and Europe. Reservoirs in Britain dried up and water was rationed. Another drought in Mid-West America in 1988 was the worst for 50 years.

Drought in Africa

For the last 20 years there has been an almost constant drought in the Sahel region of Africa. It sometimes rains between July and September, but the rain is quickly washed away, taking the soil with it. The people are unable to grow their crops or feed their animals, and thousands have died of starvation.

Dry, cracked soil in America 1988.

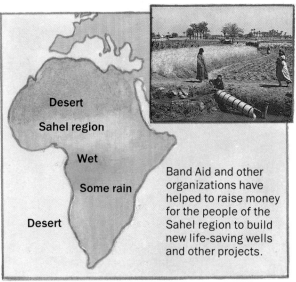

Desert

Sahel region

Wet

Some rain

Desert

Band Aid and other organizations have helped to raise money for the people of the Sahel region to build new life-saving wells and other projects.

Too much water

Floods are very common all round the world. Some cause terrible destruction. A flood caused by a cyclone in Bangladesh in 1970 killed about one million people. Other floods ruin crops and damage property. The 1976 drought in Europe was followed by floods which destroyed the Soviet grain harvest. Sudan and Bangladesh had very severe floods in 1988.

Flood in Sudan

Monsoon

In July each year in Asia there is a monsoon. This is a deluge of rain, caused by winds called the South West Monsoon. They blow over the Indian Ocean and bring rain, which is followed by a dry season. Asian farmers are geared to the monsoon and a delay of just a few weeks can cause droughts and famine.

Worst disasters this century

1900	USA: storm tide kills 6,000 people along the coast of Texas
1906	Hong Kong: typhoon strikes killing 50,000 people
1911	Yangtze River, China: floods drown 100,000 people
1925	USA: tornadoes kill 700 people in one day
1931	Yangtze River, China: floods drown 150,000 people
1939	Henan, China: floods kill one million people
1943	Bengal, India: drought leads to famine and kills one and a half million people
1952	London: smog kills over 2,500 people
1953	North Sea coastal areas: storm tide kills 2,000
1955	USA: hurricane kills 200 people
1962	Peru: avalanche buries more than 3,000 people
1963	Bangladesh: cyclone and tidal waves kill 20,000 people
1966	Florence, Italy: River Arno floods, destroying priceless works of art
1970	Bangladesh: cyclone and floods kill one million people
1975	Northeastern Africa: drought leads to famine and kills 50,000 people
1975	Umtali, Zimbabwe: lightning kills 21 people
1980+	Sahel region, Africa: drought leads to famine, killing thousands of people
1988	Sudan: torrential rain causes severe floods, thousands made homeless

And now the weather...

Every day, all round the world, hundreds of weather forecasts are given out on TV and radio, in newspapers and on telephone and computer networks. All this information comes from meteorological offices – in Britain the London Weather Centre and the main Met Office at Bracknell in Berkshire.

Weather readings from satellites, ships, planes, balloons and weather stations arrive at the meteorological office. You can find out more about this over the page.

Satellite receiving dish

Radio receiving antenna

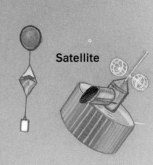
Satellite

Weather plane

Weather station

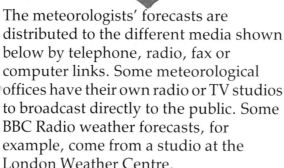

Meteorologists analyze all the readings using computers and by making special charts. By piecing together all these clues they make predictions, or forecasts, of what the weather is likely to do next. You can find out more about how this is done on pages 38-39.

Weather ship

The meteorologists' forecasts are distributed to the different media shown below by telephone, radio, fax or computer links. Some meteorological offices have their own radio or TV studios to broadcast directly to the public. Some BBC Radio weather forecasts, for example, come from a studio at the London Weather Centre.

Television

TV stations broadcast local and national weather forecasts, often using the latest computer graphics techniques.

Computer

Computer information networks, like the BBC's Ceefax service, have up-to-the-minute national forecasts.

Radio

Radio forecasts are especially useful for the merchant navy, who listen out for storm warnings at sea.

Newspapers

Newspapers often show the weather at holiday resorts around the world, as well as giving local forecasts.

Telephone

Telephone companies often give forecasts for very localized areas – useful if you are travelling.

TV maps and symbols

Most television weather maps are created on special-effects computers. The computer can show, or simulate, how clouds are expected to spread the next day, for example. The map shown below is used on BBC1.

Worldwide weather

The pictures below show how weather maps are shown in different papers around the world.

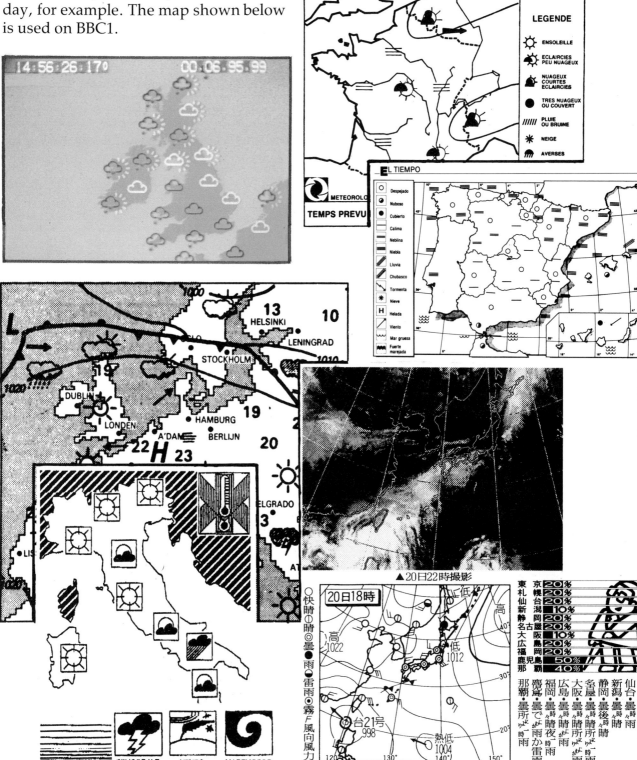

Weather watch

Weather forecasters are a bit like detectives. They are constantly piecing together clues about the state of the weather now, to work out what might happen next. The word "forecast" was first used by Britain's Chief Meteorologist, Admiral Fitzroy, in 1850. Forecasters have to keep a close watch on the weather. They make their observations using a variety of different equipment.

Gathering information

There are about 10,000 weather stations all over the world. They are linked together in a system called the World Meteorological Organization. Small stations are linked to a "trunk" of main weather centres, shown on this map.

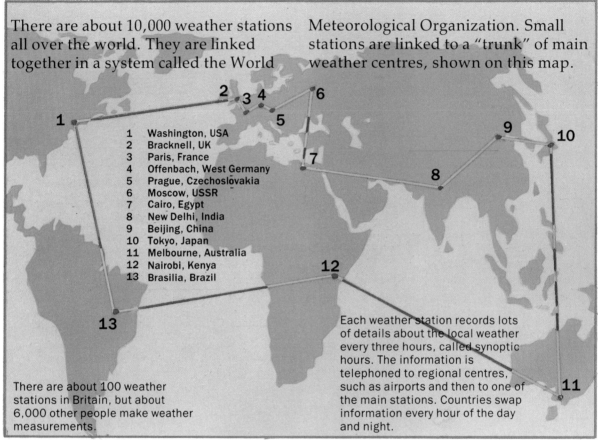

1	Washington, USA
2	Bracknell, UK
3	Paris, France
4	Offenbach, West Germany
5	Prague, Czechoslovakia
6	Moscow, USSR
7	Cairo, Egypt
8	New Delhi, India
9	Beijing, China
10	Tokyo, Japan
11	Melbourne, Australia
12	Nairobi, Kenya
13	Brasilia, Brazil

Each weather station records lots of details about the local weather every three hours, called synoptic hours. The information is telephoned to regional centres, such as airports and then to one of the main stations. Countries swap information every hour of the day and night.

There are about 100 weather stations in Britain, but about 6,000 other people make weather measurements.

What is recorded?

Outside each weather station is a box called a Stevenson screen. This shields the weather recording instruments it contains from direct sunlight.

The meteorologist records details of:

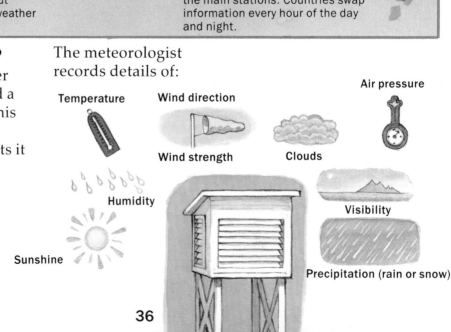

Temperature

Wind direction

Wind strength

Clouds

Air pressure

Humidity

Visibility

Sunshine

Precipitation (rain or snow)

Collecting information

Information about the weather is also gathered in other ways too. The pictures below show some of the main methods used.

Balloons

Balloons are sent about 20km up in the air every day. They carry radio transmitters and send details of temperature and humidity.

These are also called "radiosonde" balloons.

Eventually the balloon bursts and its instruments crash to the ground.

Satellites

Satellites collect information about the atmosphere which cannot be seen from the ground, such as temperature at various heights and cloud coverage over a wide area.

Radar

A network of radars track the progress of rain across the country. Each radar has a range of 200km. Colour-coded patches on the screen show the amount of rain falling.

A radar picture of showers over Britain.

Radars are also used to track the position of tornadoes.

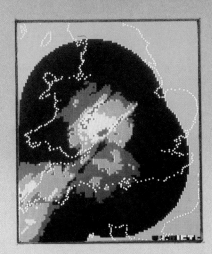

Special aircraft

There are special aircraft fitted with instruments to detect weather conditions. In the USA planes even fly through hurricanes to find out more about them. The UK Meteorological Research plane is called "Snoopy" because its instruments are in a funny nose.

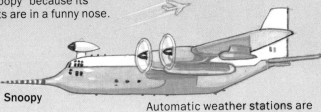

Snoopy

Automatic weather stations are also on buoys at sea and on some aircraft.

Ships and aircraft

Volunteer crews send reports to weather stations of weather conditions they observe at sea or in the air.

Automatic weather stations

These are often on remote islands, but some are in the countryside. They make automatic measurements and send them by radio or phone lines to main stations.

Forecasting

Weather forecasters piece together the information they gather from around the world, then make two sorts of forecasts – short and long range. A special map is drawn, called a synoptic chart, to predict the short range weather 24 hours ahead.

Computers are used to make quite accurate long range forecasts as much as 8 days ahead. Scientists think that by the year 2020 it will be possible to make accurate forecasts up to 14 days ahead.

Who needs a forecast?

You might want to know what the weather will be like tomorrow if you want to go to the beach, for example. But companies need accurate forecasts to help them plan their work. Each day, a country's meteorological service sells special weather information to organizations such as those shown below.

Airlines

Airlines save money on fuel by getting their pilots to avoid strong headwinds, which slow down the plane, and by flying at the best height for the weather.

Farmers

Farmers need to know the best time to sow, spray, water or harvest their crops. Pesticides, for example, are wasted if the farmer uses them just before it rains.

Construction companies

Frost spoils new concrete, rain makes earth-moving difficult and big cranes are dangerous to use in strong winds. Builders check the weather to plan what they should do.

Supermarkets

Supermarkets will buy lots of extra salad vegetables, cold drinks and ice cream if hot weather is forecast. People buy more of these things in a hot spell.

Making a forecast

The forecaster uses the latest information on pressure, wind, temperature, rainfall, cloud cover and so on to draw the synoptic chart. This gives the best clues about what might happen next. The synoptic chart uses isobars – points of equal pressure linked together in lines – to tell you about lows, highs and fronts.

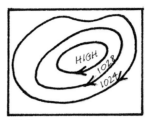 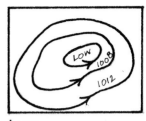

Highs

High-pressure areas, called anticylones, bring dry, settled weather. Any winds blow clockwise in these areas.

Lows

Low-pressure areas, called depressions, bring cloud and rain. The winds blow anti-clockwise in these areas.

Fronts

Fronts are boundaries between different masses of air. There are four main kinds of airmass, shown on the map below, which are named after the kind of climate they come from. The weather is often very unsettled near fronts, with rain and clouds. There are three sorts of fronts: warm, cold and occluded.

Air masses

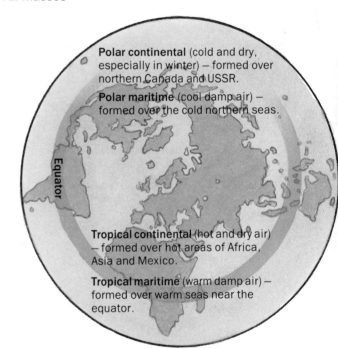

Polar continental (cold and dry, especially in winter) – formed over northern Canada and USSR.

Polar maritime (cool damp air) – formed over the cold northern seas.

Equator

Tropical continental (hot and dry air) – formed over hot areas of Africa, Asia and Mexico.

Tropical maritime (warm damp air) – formed over warm seas near the equator.

Warm fronts

Warm fronts are when warm air advances and rides up over cold air.

From above   **From the side**

These symbols mean warm front

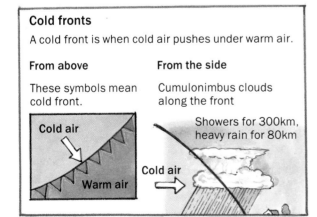

Rain or snow for about 250km.

Warm air

Cold air

Cold fronts

A cold front is when cold air pushes under warm air.

From above   **From the side**

These symbols mean cold front.

Cumulonimbus clouds along the front

Cold air

Warm air

Cold air

Showers for 300km, heavy rain for 80km

Occluded fronts

Occluded fronts are when cold air has advanced on warm air and lifted it.

From above   **From the side**

These symbols mean occluded front.

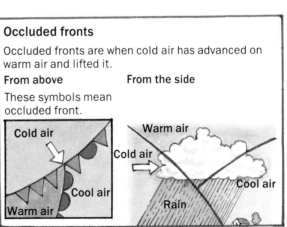

Cold air

Cool air

Warm air

Warm air

Cold air

Cool air

Rain

Weather station

You might like to set up your own weather station and keep a record of the weather. Here is how to make the equipment you need to measure wind direction and speed, temperature and pressure. There is a rain gauge to make on page 20.

It is a good idea to take readings at the same time each day, otherwise it will be difficult to compare the results from one day to another.

Wind direction

You can measure wind direction with this simple wind vane. It works just like a weather cock on a church tower.

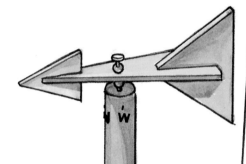

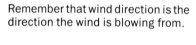

Remember that wind direction is the direction the wind is blowing from.

on page 20.

You need:

Some sheets of balsa wood (or thin plywood if you want your wind vane to last longer).

A nail

2 plastic beads (nail must fit holes loosely)

Balsa glue

Hammer

Craft knife

A compass

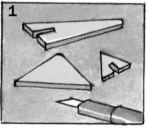

1 Cut the pieces for the wind vane as shown above.

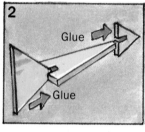

2 Glue the pieces together as shown.
Glue
Glue

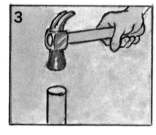

3 Find a wooden fence post, or bang one into the ground.

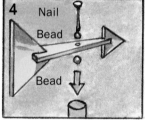

4 Nail
Bead
Bead
Fix the wind vane to the post as shown.

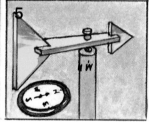

5 Mark north where south should be, east where west should be, and so on.

6 The arrow will point towards the direction the wind is blowing from.

Temperature

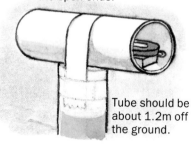

Air flows through the open ends.

Tube should be about 1.2m off the ground.

To take the temperature you need an ordinary household thermometer, but it must be kept in a shaded place outside. Meteorologists use a special shade called a Stevenson screen (see page 36). You can make a simple shade to protect your thermometer from direct sunlight.

You need:

Thermometer

Plastic bottle

1.5m wooden post

2 matchboxes

White emulsion paint and brush

Scissors

Hammer   Sticky tape

1 Cut the ends off the bottle to make a tube.

2 Place the thermometer inside the tube, balanced on matchboxes.

3 Paint the tube white. This will reflect direct sunlight.

4 Bang the post into the ground and tape the tube to it. Remove the thermometer to take a reading.

Air pressure

Meteorologists use a barometer to measure air pressure (see page 15). This simple barometer will detect whether the pressure is rising or falling.

You need:
A clear tall plastic bottle
Brick
Ink or powder paint
Water
Sticky tape
Sticky label
Shallow plastic dish
Someone to help

1 Colour some cold water with ink or powder paint and three-quarters fill the bottle.

2 Put your finger over the bottle and turn it upside down into the dish. Keep the bottle upright.

3 Tape the bottle to the brick as shown and mark the water level with the sticky label.

4 The water level rises as the air pressure rises, and falls as the pressure falls.

Wind speed

Wind speed is measured with an instrument called an anemometer. You can make a simple one of your own quite easily.

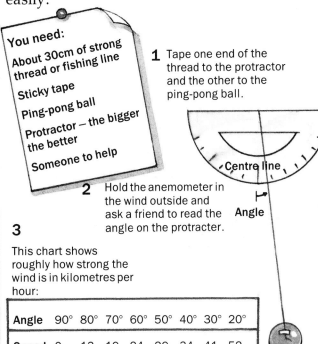

You need:
About 30cm of strong thread or fishing line
Sticky tape
Ping-pong ball
Protractor – the bigger the better
Someone to help

1 Tape one end of the thread to the protractor and the other to the ping-pong ball.

2 Hold the anemometer in the wind outside and ask a friend to read the angle on the protracter.

3 This chart shows roughly how strong the wind is in kilometres per hour:

Angle	90°	80°	70°	60°	50°	40°	30°	20°
Speed in kph	0	13	19	24	29	34	41	52

Weather notebook

You could record the weather each day in a notebook drawn out like the one below. Take notes on wind direction and speed, temperature, pressure, rainfall, sunshine and cloud cover.

Weather long ago

About 20,000 years ago, most of northern Britain was covered in a thick sheet of ice hundreds of metres thick – the last ice age. Since then, the climate has become warmer and the ice has melted to cover just the north and south poles. Scientists think that we are now in a warm part of another ice age, which could last 50,000 years or so.

Water levels

As the Earth's climate slowly changes over many centuries, the ice at the poles gets thicker or thinner. The sea has risen about 100m over the last 10,000 years as the ice has melted. There is enough ice left at the poles to make the sea rise another 100m. This would be deep enough to flood London, New York, Sydney and many other low-lying towns and cities.

The last 7,000 years

5,000-2,000 BC

The weather was much warmer than it is now. This lasted until Roman times. The weather was warm enough in Britain, for example, for the occupying Romans to be able to grow grapes.

1600-1800 AD

A cold period occurred called the "little ice age". Glaciers, sheets of ice on mountains, got thicker, and rivers in Europe froze over every winter. The ice on the Thames was so thick, that "frost fairs" were held.

1800-1900 AD

The temperature began to rise again. The bodies of climbers who had fallen to their deaths in Victorian times were found as mountain glaciers melted a little.

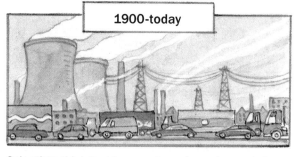

1900-today

Scientists think that temperatures have dropped about 0·5°C. Pollution is now threatening the natural changes. Oddly, 1987 was the warmest year worldwide this century.

Why does the climate change?

Natural changes in the world's climate are always gradually taking place. There are many reasons for this, but scientists think that things such as volcanic eruptions and wobbles in the Earth's tilt are mainly to blame.

Wobbles

The Earth orbits the Sun at an angle called its axis. Sometimes the planet wobbles on its axis and this affects the amount of sunlight reaching the surface.

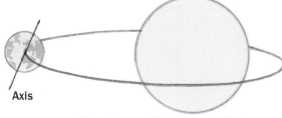

Axis

This shape of this orbit is called an ellipse.

Volcanoes

Millions of tonnes of dust are thrown into the atmosphere when a large volcano erupts. In 1883 the Krakatoa volcano exploded and the dust stayed in the air for three years. This affected the climate because less sun could shine through the darkened skies.

Testing change

Scientists have different ways of finding out what the climate used to be like.

Fossils

Fossils sometimes contain things such as seeds which give clues about the kind of climate at the time the fossil was formed.

Tree rings

Each ring on a tree is a record of the kind of weather at the time the ring was formed. Thick rings show that the weather was warm that year, for example.

Fossilized remains of tree stumps showing their annual growth rings have been found.

Historical records

The ancient Romans, Chinese and Greeks kept weather records and also noted when crops were harvested. Detailed records have been kept for Europe and the USA since about 1700 AD.

End of the dinosaurs

Some scientists think that the dinosaurs died out about 65 million years ago because of changes in the climate. One idea is that a meteor struck the Earth, causing a giant dust cloud which blocked the Sun's heat. Dinosaurs are thought to have been cold blooded, so they would have frozen to death.

Krakatoa, between Java and Sumatra.

What is happening to the weather?

Many adults remember the weather being different in their childhood, compared to how it is now, with snow at Christmas and long, hot summers. Is this just memories of happy times, or is the weather really changing? Most scientists think that it is, although they don't all agree what kind of changes will happen or what the causes are. Many people believe that pollution is to blame, but there are different theories about the effects of the world's car fumes, power station smoke and industrial waste.

Holes in the sky

In 1985, scientists at the British Antarctic Survey discovered that there were thin patches, or "holes", in the ozone layer of the atmosphere over Antarctica. Ozone is a protective gas cloud 10-60km up in the atmosphere. It keeps out harmful rays from the sun and prevents the Earth from getting too hot. The holes are thought to be caused by too many waste gases called chlorofluorocarbons – CFCs for short – escaping from aerosols, plastic foam cartons and many other industrial products.

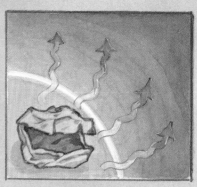

CFCs escape from burger cartons when they are crushed.

What does it mean for the weather?

The earth seems to be getting hotter – perhaps as a result of extra heat from the sun getting through the damaged ozone layer. This could mean that the polar ice caps will melt, and that rainfall and wind patterns will change. Latest forecasts are that average world temperatures could increase by as much as 5°C over the next 100 years.

Greenhouse effect

Since the industrial revolution in the 18th century, there has been a 25% increase in the amount of carbon dioxide in the atmosphere. Carbon dioxide is a gas. The extra amount has come from things such as factory smoke, car exhausts and the burning down of the world's rain forests.

The carbon dioxide forms a cloud around the earth which allows the sun's rays through, but prevents the heat from escaping back into space. This acts like the glass in a greenhouse by trapping the warm air inside, making the earth hotter and hotter.

What does it mean for the weather?

The polar ice caps are likely to melt over many years, but meanwhile the weather could be very unpredictable. Changes in rainfall patterns over the next 100 years could make northern Europe wetter and southern Europe and Africa even drier than it is now.

El Nino

El Nino is a current of water in the southern Pacific ocean. It is usually very cold, but every few years it warms up – nobody knows why. Some scientists think that when this happens, the weather behaves very oddly in the Far East and western USA. These scientists argue that El Nino is more important than the greenhouse effect or holes in the ozone layer.

What does it mean for the weather?

There is not much to prove that El Nino has any effect in Europe, but some people think that Asian and American weather becomes more extreme when El Nino heats up.

Acid rain

Waste gases, such as sulphur dioxide and nitrogen oxides, and small particles from power stations and car exhausts, are dissolved in rainwater. This turns the rain into an acid – often as strong as lemon juice. Pollution from one country is often blown by the wind to make acid rain in a neighbouring country.

What does it mean for the weather?

Acid rain does not affect the weather directly, but it does kill trees, poison lakes and damage crops. Trees absorb the gas carbon dioxide, so less trees means more carbon dioxide in the atmosphere, adding to the greenhouse effect. Acid rain also destroys buildings because it eats into the stonework.

A forest devastated by acid rain.

Weather records

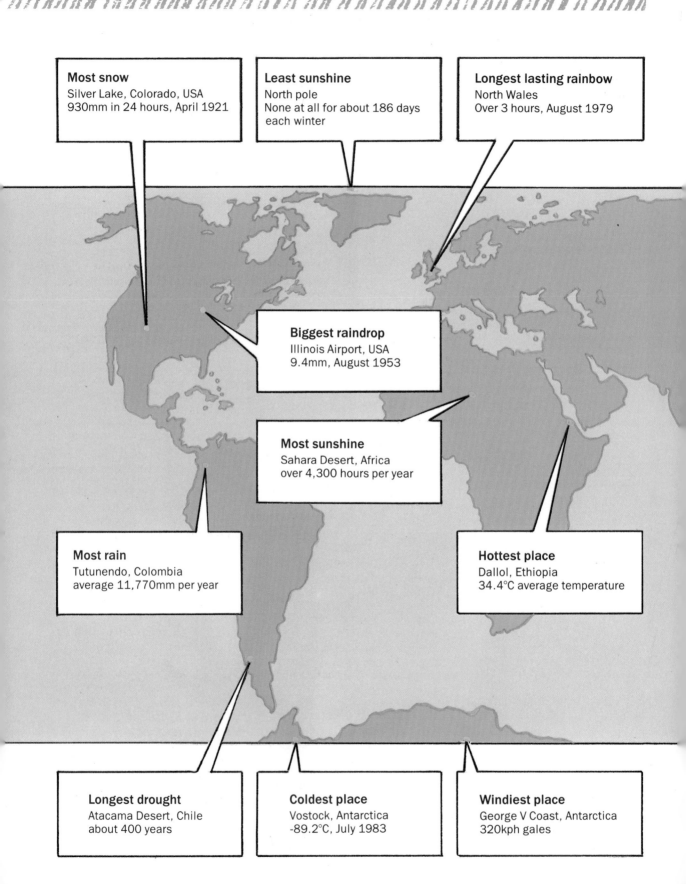

Most snow
Silver Lake, Colorado, USA
930mm in 24 hours, April 1921

Least sunshine
North pole
None at all for about 186 days
each winter

Longest lasting rainbow
North Wales
Over 3 hours, August 1979

Biggest raindrop
Illinois Airport, USA
9.4mm, August 1953

Most sunshine
Sahara Desert, Africa
over 4,300 hours per year

Most rain
Tutunendo, Colombia
average 11,770mm per year

Hottest place
Dallol, Ethiopia
34.4°C average temperature

Longest drought
Atacama Desert, Chile
about 400 years

Coldest place
Vostock, Antarctica
-89.2°C, July 1983

Windiest place
George V Coast, Antarctica
320kph gales

Weather words

Acid rain: Rain which is a very weak acid. It is too weak to harm people, but may damage trees and buildings.

Air mass: A region of warm or cold, moist or dry air.

Air pressure: The weight of the Earth's atmosphere pressing down on the surface.

Anemometer: An instrument for measuring wind speed and direction.

Anticyclone: Another name for a high pressure area.

Atmosphere: The gases surrounding the Earth.

Barometer: An instrument for measuring atmospheric pressure.

Beaufort scale: A scale of wind speeds.

Climate: The weather over a period of time in one place.

Cold front: The boundary between two airmasses where the cold air is advancing. Usually brings a spell of rain followed by cooler but brighter weather.

Condensation: When water vapour cools and turns into water.

Cyclone: Another name for a low pressure area, but normally used only in tropical areas.

Depression: Another name for a low pressure area.

Dew point: The temperature at which the water vapour in the air condenses to form droplets.

Greenhouse effect: The warming of the Earth caused by a cloud of pollution preventing the Sun's heat from escaping to space.

Hail: A particle of ice which sometimes are formed in cumulonimbus clouds.

Humidity: The amount of moisture in the air

Hurricane: A very powerful swirling storm.

Isobars: Lines drawn on a map linking points of equal pressure.

Lightning: An electrical charge which jumps from cloud to cloud or from a cloud to the ground.

Occluded front: A band of cloud and rain – like a mixture of a cold and a warm front.

Rain: Liquid water drops falling from the sky. Called drizzle if the drops are tiny.

Shower: Rain falling from a cumulonimbus cloud. Usually lasts less than an hour.

Snow: Ice crystals falling from the sky. Called hail if the crystals are joined as hard lumps.

Thermometer: An instrument for measuring temperature (how hot or cold it is).

Thunderstorm: A storm with thunder and lightning.

Stevenson screen: A white box which protects weather instruments from the direct heat of the Sun.

Warm front: Boundary between two airmasses where the warm air is advancing. Usually brings a spell of rain followed by warmer, moist air.

Water vapour: Water in the form of a gas.

Wind vane: A simple instrument for measuring wind direction.

Most rainy days
Mt. Wai-'ale-'ale, Hawaii
up to 350 days per year

Biggest hailstone
Gopalganj, Bangladesh
1.02kg, April 1986

Index

Published by BBC Educational Publishing,
a division of BBC Enterprises Limited,
Woodlands, 80 Wood Lane, London W12 0TT
First published 1989
Reprinted 1989, 1990, 1992 (twice)

© 1989 Tony Potter

Devised and produced by Tony Potter for BBC Enterprises Limited

Paperback ISBN: 0 563 21427 9
Hardback ISBN: 0 563 21428 7

Printed in Great Britain by Purnell Book Production Ltd.

Picture credits
cover (left) Colin Crane (right) Tony Potter **p2** Earth Satellite Corporation/Science Photo Library **p4** B. Angrove/Barnaby's Picture Library **p8** (top) Topham Picture Library (bottom) Topham Picture Library **p10** (bottom left) Chris Gilbert (bottom right) Topham Picture Library **p12** F. Alan Wood **p.13** (bottom left) Topham Picture Library (bottom right) Topham Picture Library **p18** Tony Potter **p19**(top left, centre right) Dick File **p22** C.J. Richards **p25** (top) T.A.M. Bradbury (bottom) Chris Gilbert **p28** Australian Information Service/Frank Lane Picture Agency **p29** (bottom left) Chris Gilbert (right) Colin Crane **p31** Topham Picture Library **p32** (left) Topham Picture Library (right) Topham Picture Library (bottom) Topham Picture Library **p35** (top) BBC/L'Unita/El Pais/Le Monde/De Telegraaf **p36** Crown **p38** (centre left) Tony Potter (centre right) G. Holman (bottom left and right) Tony Potter **p45** Chris Rose/ICCE

Typeset by TDR, Dartford, England
Origination by Dot Gradations, England

crickets

sunbirds

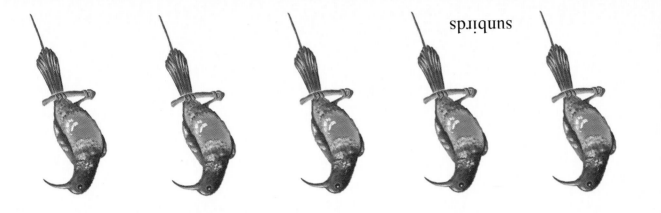

butterflies

lizards

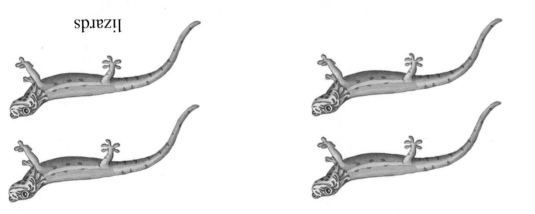

hen

mice

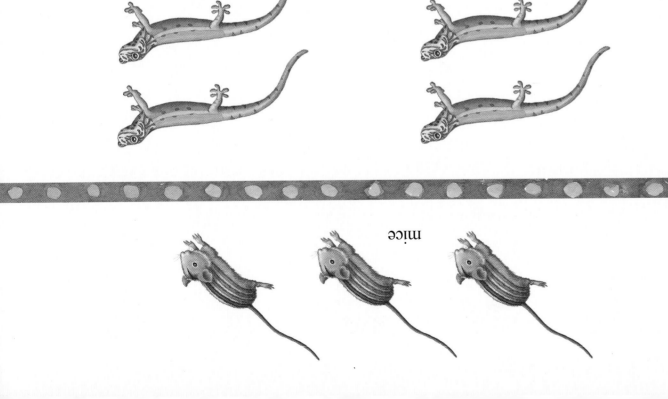

5.2010

hen

butterflies

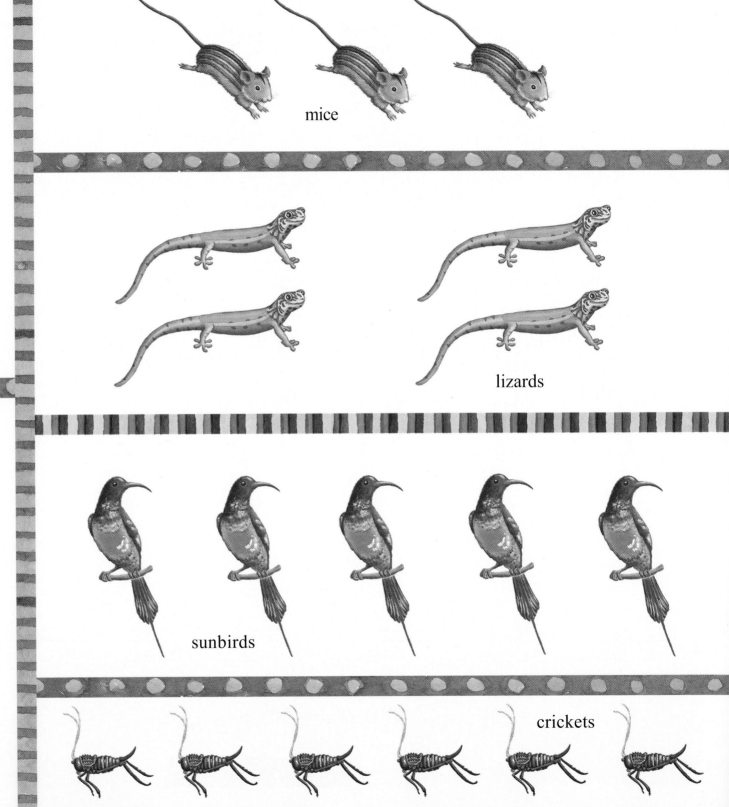

mice

lizards

sunbirds

crickets